This is NOT a spelling mistake — it's her name!

This notebook is dedicated to
→ Liisa,
because she liked the first one so much,
and to Journal Writers Everywhere.

This means no cheating, no stealing, no copycatting — make your own notebook with your own ideas. (or ask me about copying mine.)

TRICYCLE PRESS
P.O. BOX 7123
Berkeley, California 94707

Book Design by Amelia

That means Nicole, Anna, and Laura — hats off to them!

an award-winning designer — I'm NOT kidding!

Her again?

Yeah!

Library of Congress Cataloging-in-Publication Data

Moss, Marissa.
Amelia Writes Again / by Marissa Moss (and who else? me, Amelia!)
p. cm.
Summary: A ten-year-old draws and writes about her daily life in the journal she receives for her birthday.
ISBN 1-883672-42-2
[1. Family life — Fiction. 2. Schools — Fiction. 3. Diaries — Fiction.]
I. Title.
PZ7.M8535Ak 1996
[Fic] — dc20

95-52874
CIP
AC

It is too true!

First Tricycle Press Printing, 1996
manufactured in Singapore

secret code

(wink wink)
only those who know the code can read this notebook.

far, far away

3   4   5   6 — 00   99   98   97

This is my beautiful, new, BLANK notebook, waiting for me to fill it with words and drawings. But I feel as blank and empty as these pages. I mean, I just turned 10 exciting years old, but I feel exactly the same as when I was 9. And I look the same,

same brain, same ideas, same thoughts

me

same old scar from when Cleo threw a toy teapot at me — that's my stupid sister's idea of a tea party!

ears are still not pierced (not till I'm 16, says mom)

same dip under my nose — what is this thing called anyway, and what's it for? to funnel snot into your mouth when you have a runny nose?

Miss Know-It-All Cleo. If she knows so much, how come she can't eat pizza without getting it all over her face? I call her Cheezy chin.

I still had a good birthday, but I expected SOMETHING would change. I thought ten was close to teen — almost a teenager. It's not.

piece o' pizza

gooey, gluey cheese

gooey, gluey chin

Cleo says no matter how old I am, I'll always be a jerky little sister. And she'll always get to do things first. But she's wrong.

souvenir stamped penny from Space World ←

lunar surface— not swiss cheese ↙

I got to go to Space World _first_, for my birthday. Just me, Mom, and Leah. The best part was the Lunar Landing Ride. When Cleo asked what it was like, I said she'd have to find out for herself, _if_ she ever gets to go.

ticket stub from Space World ↑

postcard from Gift Shop →

SPACE WORLD

I bought this postcard just to put in my new notebook. But when I did, Leah asked if she could see what I write in here. I said maybe. She may be my new best friend, but I don't know if I want her to see my private thoughts and drawings. What if she laughs at me or thinks I'm dumb?

One thing is sure, I _NEVER_ want Cleo to see what's in here.

Special sensitized magnetic strip that sets off Cleo-alarm if she touches any part of this notebook ↓

my new paint set

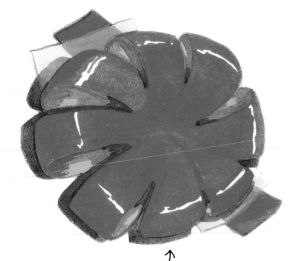

my new brush

Anyway, guess who gave me this notebook for my birthday? Not Nadia. She sent me a beautiful watercolor set with a great brush. Not Leah. She gave me a charm bracelet to match her own. Not even Mom. She gave me a Walkman.

ribbon from Nadia's present— she's still my best friend, even far away, but Leah's my best friend, too, now. Can you have 2 best friends? Isn't one always best-est? I know Nadia better, but Leah's here, which is definitely better, except when she asks to read my notebook

← spilled grape juice — NOT! it's purple paint from my new paint set

birthday card from Nadia — she drew it herself

↑ birthday card from Leah

It was Cleo!!! She said now I could write something NICE about her for a change.

But you hafta write good stuff about me.

Thanks!

She didn't say EVERYTHING I wrote about her had to be nice. Just <u>something</u>.

Here goes: Cleo does have 1 good thing about her — her hands. She has long, elegant fingers and she doesn't chew on her fingernails the way I do.

fingerprint

plate of spaghetti

← hairy bug

↑ furball

Some hands have short, stubby fingers. I call them Glove Hands.

↑ Glove Hand

← witch hand or claw

Some hands are all bony.

you can count on a limp handshake with this hand

droopy, drippy hand

hand with pinchy fingers — I call these Twig Hands

fingers going sight-seeing — oh, no! I drew 611 fingers! what a sight to see!

Some hands seem smart. Others seem dumb. And this has nothing to do with whether the people they belong to are stupid or smart. It's just the way the hands look. Wide-awake or droopy, itchy or snooty, pinchy or thick.

fingers going for a walk

fingers meaning business

I like to watch deaf people's hands. It's like watching expressions fly across someone's face or hearing feelings.

bunny fingers hopping around

duck fingers making shadows on a wall

There's a kid in my class, Eli. He has great hands, but better than that, he has the most amazing gestures. It's like his hands are having their own conversation while he's talking.

It's hard to show movement in a still drawing, but it's kind of like this

Don't interrupt me!

I'm not!

I keep trying to start my math homework, but I always get distracted by my hand that's doing the writing, and then I get distracted by the numbers.

Numbers each have their own personalities.

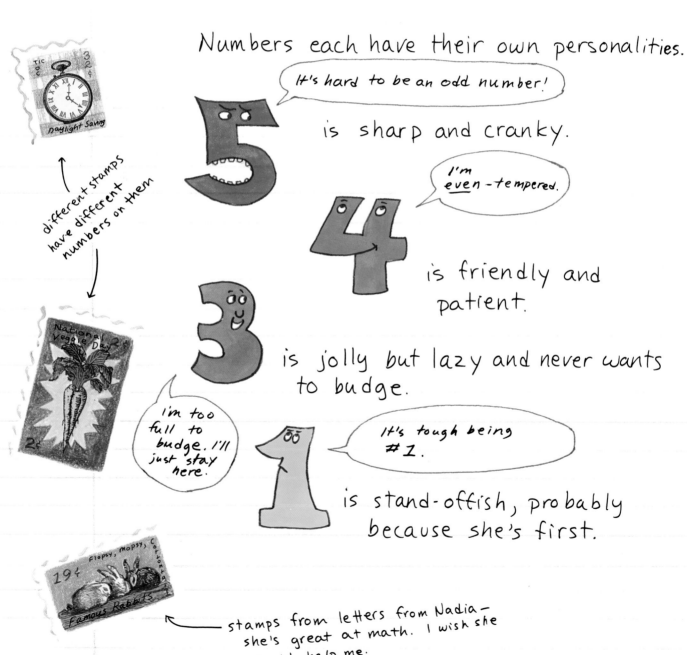

It's hard to be an odd number!

5 is sharp and cranky.

I'm even-tempered.

4 is friendly and patient.

3 is jolly but lazy and never wants to budge.

I'm too full to budge. I'll just stay here.

It's tough being #1.

1 is stand-offish, probably because she's first.

different stamps have different numbers on them

stamps from letters from Nadia— she's great at math. I wish she could help me.

more Nadia stamps

Before I know it, I'm telling myself a story about the numbers in the problem.

Like  is all mad at

for being a copycat (only upside down and backwards, which is even worse as far as 5 is concerned), so the 2 of them are hissing at each other when they're supposed to stand together and be divided by 6 ½.

But  is too busy taking care of baby

stinky diapoo

who needs his diaper changed, to pay any attention to

You think you're so smart! I'm more than you! I count more!

Yeah? Well, more isn't always better. You can be more of a jerk, so there!

Then Mom says it's dinnertime, and

My paper is still blank. That is, there are no answers written down, although there are lots of doodles in the margins. Last night's homework ended up looking like a map made by an alien instead of a math worksheet.

Sometimes this happens during a quiz, which is really bad. I end up handing in a no-answer quiz.

numbers refusing to cooperate and running away, leaving me with a big, fat

Hmmm... take a left at Venus, right at Mars, straight past Pluto, and where are you?

Mr. Nudel's big teacher desk

me, sinking into the floor

blank quiz

scribbled math worksheet

Mr. Nudel says I just have to concentrate, he knows I can do it. I know I can do it, too, so if we both know I can do it, why do I actually have to do it?

Now, Amelia, use that old noodle.

in cartoons, men don't have eyelashes — in real life, they do

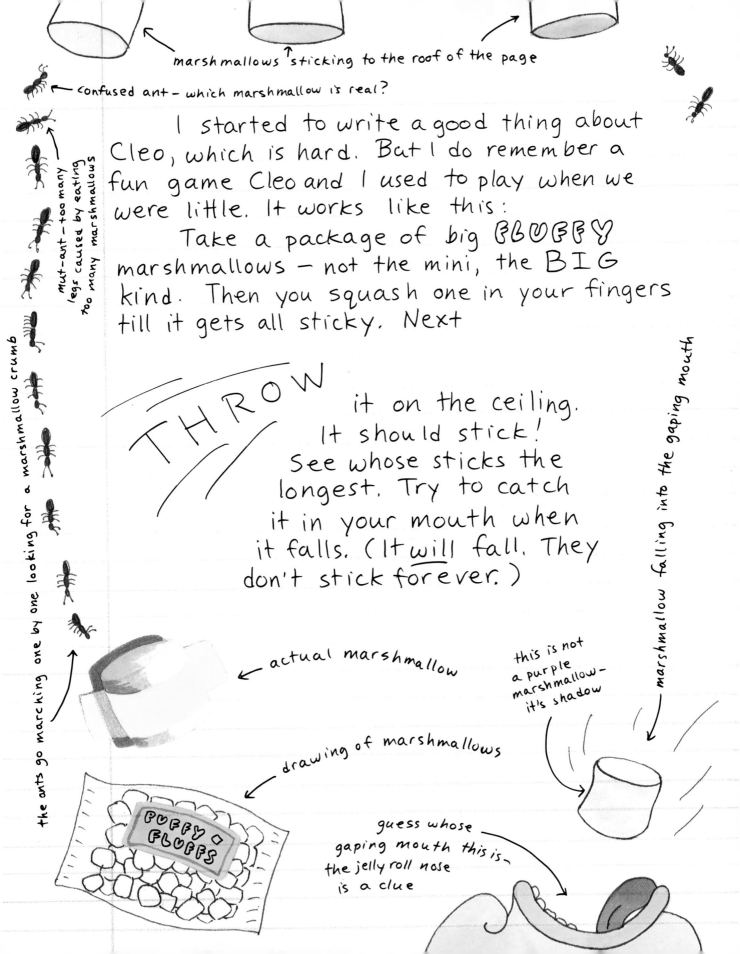

marshmallows sticking to the roof of the page

confused ant - which marshmallow is real?

Mut-ant - too many legs caused by eating too many marshmallows

the ants go marching one by one looking for a marshmallow crumb

I started to write a good thing about Cleo, which is hard. But I do remember a fun game Cleo and I used to play when we were little. It works like this:

Take a package of big FLUFFY marshmallows — not the mini, the BIG kind. Then you squash one in your fingers till it gets all sticky. Next

THROW it on the ceiling. It should stick! See whose sticks the longest. Try to catch it in your mouth when it falls. (It will fall. They don't stick forever.)

marshmallow falling into the gaping mouth

← actual marshmallow

drawing of marshmallows

this is not a purple marshmallow — it's shadow

PUFFY FLUFFS

guess whose gaping mouth this is — the jelly roll nose is a clue

Once, we were way too noisy, and Mom walked into the room. Luckily, the marshmallows were all stuck to the ceiling and she didn't look up and see them. (Who looks at ceilings anyway? NO ONE!)

ceiling

marshmallows

about to drop— oh, no!

what's all this noise about? what's going on here?

Nothing.

Nothing.

marshmallow in cheek making a lump — I hope Mom doesn't notice

sorry, Mom, I didn't mean to make you fat

Sometimes Cleo CAN be fun, but not often — I think the marshmallows were her idea

bag of marshmallows behind Cleo's back

Just as she left, they started to drop! We were sure lucky none fell on her head.

sticky marshmallow

hairy marshmallow

imagine washing marshmallow out of your hair— yuucch!

chopsticks are no easier for me at 10 than at 9 — does anything change?

last night I got this fortune in my fortune cookie — too true!

A friendship is testing you.

I told Leah about the marshmallow game. I thought she would laugh, but she's still mad at me.

"When are you going to show me your notebook?" she's always asking now. "What's the big deal? Am I your friend or not?"

She is my friend. Part of me wants to show it to her. But part of me doesn't.

rice falling time to use a fork

me fighting myself over whether or not I should show this to Leah

Today was really terrible. Leah wouldn't even eat lunch with me. She said if I can't be honest with her, I'm not much of a friend. Is keeping some things private the same as being dishonest?

my lonely lunch

wilted lettuce and cheese sandwich

bruised apple

crumbled cookies

nothing tasted good

I thought yesterday was bad, but now a HORRIBLE, AWFUL thing has happened.

Much, much worse than any fight with Leah.

There was a big fire at our school last night, and the fire department says it was arson. That means someone set it ON PURPOSE!!

I heard a lot of sirens, but I didn't know it was my school till I got there this morning.

← piece of charred wood, probably from a desk

There was a crowd of reporters and yellow CAUTION tape across one whole wing of the school. That wing was all black and crumbly like slices of burnt

this was very hard to draw — a mess just looks like a mess

CAUTION CAUTION CAUTION CAUTION CAUTION CAUTION CAUTION CAUTION CAUTION

toast with bites taken out, and it smelled smoky like the time Mom left a potholder on the stove by mistake.

mr. Nudel   Leah↑   max   Mrs. Kravitz, the music teacher

↑
Mom's burnt potholder

First thing, instead of the Pledge of Allegiance or anything, we were all herded into the cafeteria, and Ms. Bell, the principal, told us that somebody had set fire to our school, but no one was hurt, and the creep who did it was somebody

she didn't say CREEP exactly — she said arsonist — that means CREEP!!

Ms. Bell — her fingers held the podium tight, tight →

I always thought protesters used signs or petitions or sit-ins — stuff like that — NOT fires!!

protesting something, but we're not sure what, and we're not to worry.

what, me worry? OF COURSE I worry!

And it will take a long time to rebuild, and portables will be set up next week.

portable classrooms rushing to us, even this minute

Then we went on a tour of the burned part so we could all see what it looked like. What it looked like was terrible! Burnt books, papers, parts of desks and bulletin boards.

The burned part was the first and second grades. Not my classroom. I'm really glad about that, at least. But I feel kind of bad about feeling glad. I can't help it, I a_m glad. Is that bad?

bits of broken glass everywhere

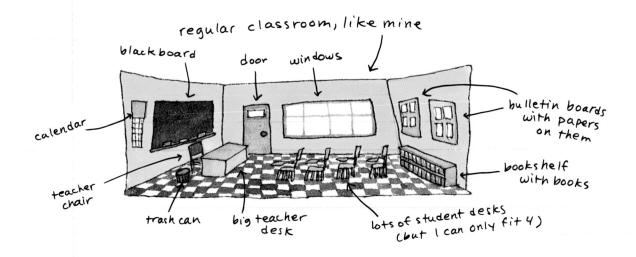

regular classroom, like mine

blackboard

door windows

calendar

bulletin boards with papers on them

teacher chair

bookshelf with books

trash can

big teacher desk

lots of student desks (but I can only fit 4)

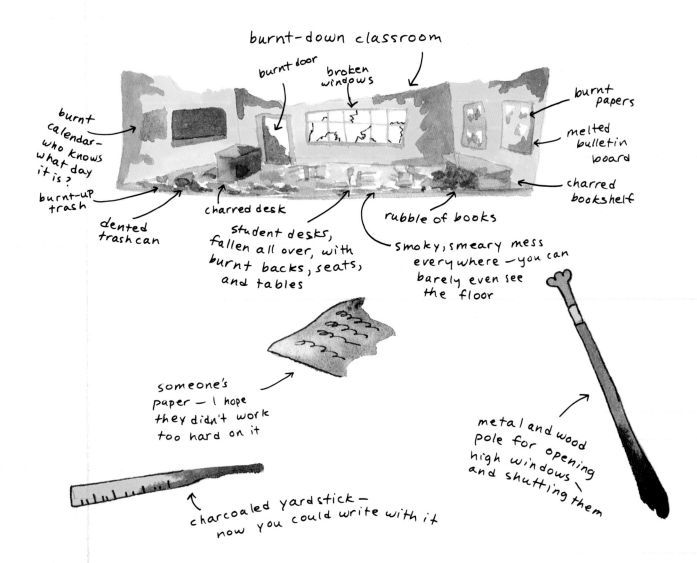

burnt-down classroom

burnt door

broken windows

burnt papers

burnt calendar— who knows what day it is?

melted bulletin board

burnt-up trash

charred bookshelf

dented trash can

charred desk

rubble of books

Student desks, fallen all over, with burnt backs, seats, and tables

smoky, smeary mess everywhere —you can barely even see the floor

someone's paper — I hope they didn't work too hard on it

metal and wood pole for opening high windows and shutting them

charcoaled yardstick— now you could write with it

The worst part was Ms. Rooney's classroom. She had brought her own comfy armchair to school, her own books, her own light-up globe. All that stuff was ruined.

black patches all over

springs springing out

torn-up bits

I saw her sitting in her blackened chair with the sunflowers on it. She was crying, but not making a sound. It made me feel awful to see her.

I wrote Nadia a long letter about the fire, and I'm writing about it here in my notebook, too, but I still can't get it out of my head.

Sometimes getting things outside of me and onto paper helps. Not this time. I keep seeing Ms. Rooney with the tears running down her cheeks.

trying to mail my troubles away

To: Nadia

Leah

me

At least Leah's not mad at me anymore. Or maybe she's forgotten about my notebook. No one can think of anything but the fire.

Even Cleo has been nice.

me watching T.V.
on the nubby green rug

Cleo bringing me cinnamon
toast and hot chocolate

But the yellow
tape is still up.
I won't feel
better until
it's gone.

 jack

ducky barrette

bus token

die (it's not dead— it's one dice)

Yesterday the workers started to rebuild the school, and I got a great idea. I told Mr. Nudel, and he told Ms. Bell, and she thinks my idea is great, too!

rubber ball

They said  YES!

button

So this is what we get to do:

When the workers pour new cement for a new pavement in front of the new classrooms, each kid is supposed to bring a treasure from home, like a plastic dinosaur, a button, a seashell — anything!
And we each get to put our treasure in the wet cement and write our initials next to it.

tiny plastic clothespin

little toy baby bottle

heart bead

metal car

wind-up chattering teeth

broken geode

plastic dinosaur

rubbery snake

ring
A.E.

E.D.

R.F.
bubble wand

A.S.
heart cookie cutter

dice (2 die, that is!)
B.B.

chess marker

worry doll— no more worries!
M.M

S.S.
little lock

N.G.
watermelon eraser

E.S.
← battery, probably dead

W.A.
← witch finger

little metal chain
D.F.

seashell
A.P.

M.Y.
polished rock

mystery key—no one remembers what it unlocks
H.S.

rubber fly →
H.T.

E.K.
apple seeds

C.E.
acorn

plastic fish
D.L.

G.L.
screw

wooden doll
S.M.

M.K.
doggy barrette

birthday candle— another chance to make a wish!
L.P.

J.B.T.

wishbone— make a wish!
B.N.

marble
A.J.

pencil sharpener
F.I.

good luck horseshoe magnet

parcheesi marker
T.T.

← checker

iron marker from monopoly game →

my marker, making a different kind of mark!

It was great! I put in a marker because I like to draw and write so much. (It was out of ink, anyway.) Leah put in a charm from her charm bracelet. One first-grader put in a tooth he'd just lost. (He said he still got money from the tooth fairy for it.)

The last person to put something in was Ms. Rooney. She put in her good-luck penny to bring the school and all of us good luck.

Leah's charm, an angel riding a dove

Mrs. Kravitz, the music teacher, put in a finger cymbal

tiny tooth

1995 D

Ms. Jenko, the P.E. teacher, put in her whistle

Ms. Bell put in a jingle bell

shiny, good-luck penny

← Mr. Nudel put in a dry noodle

And for the first time since the fire,
I saw Ms. Rooney smile.

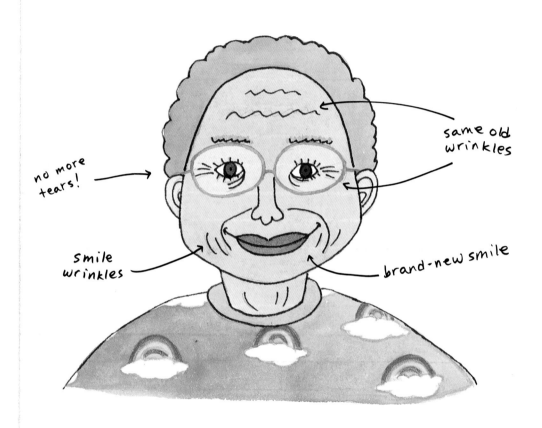

I wrote Nadia about my idea, and I drew her a great picture of our new sidewalk. She wrote me back right away.

Nadia's **letter**—actually, it's a postcard

Lake Cowabunga

Dear Amelia,
    I got your great letter and drawing. I sure wish I could put a treasure in the cement, too. I'd put in a bead from my necklace that matches your necklace. I'd put it right next to your marker. I can't wait to visit and see how everything looks. Maybe for winter vacation, Mom ~~says~~. Your friend forever,
♡♡♡♡ Nadia ♡♡♡♡

27¢ say cheese
In praise of cheese

2¢ LANCELOT

Amelia,
my best friend
564 North Homerest
Oopa, Oregon
97881

this is Nadia the way I remember her — it's been a few months since I moved away, but I still miss her

I guess I'll always miss her

special delivery stamps for special letters, specially delivered

some stamps sure have strange pictures on them

Things are beginning to feel normal again at school. And they caught the arsonist. (CREEEEP!!) It was some man who wanted to protest against our government. I can't figure out how burning down our school sends a message to the government. Couldn't he just send a letter? Or if he was really in a hurry, a fax?

letter to the president, like Mom always writes when she doesn't like a law or something— she writes tons of letters, to Congress, to the president, to anyone she thinks should listen

bushy president eyebrows

baggy president eyes

the President
the White House
Washington, D.C.

pencil Power 32

PRIVATE!!
for presidential eyes only — official U.S. Business!

I'm so happy everything is all taken care of — the arsonist (still a CREEPULAR CREEPACIOUS CREEP!) and the school.

Now I don't have to worry anymore. Now I can think about writing stories again. If I can think of any. Maybe when I have a story (if it's a good one), I can show my notebook to Leah.

I have an  already!

A Good Luck Story

A girl found a shiny new penny on the sidewalk. She picked it up for good luck and named it Patty so she could call it Pretty Patty Penny (or P.P.P. for short). She put Patty in her pocket, but she didn't know her pocket had a hole in it. The penny fell out, and with it went all of her good luck.

Bad things started to happen to the girl. She dropped her books in a puddle. She punched the tetherball and it hit her

hole in pocket

girl whistling because she feels so lucky

schoolbook

lunch box

"Ouch!" said Pretty Patty Penny. "Being bonked on the head is not lucky for me!"

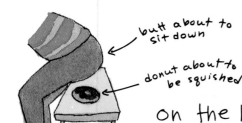

butt about to sit down

donut about to be squished

on the head. (ouch!) She sat on her chocolate donut at lunchtime.

Pretty Patty Penny wasn't having much luck either. A seagull tried to eat her but spit her out. A dog almost peed on her, but she rolled away just in time. Then a lady in pointy high heels stepped on her. Could things get worse?

touch-down!

frosting oozing out

Yuucch!

Yuucch! seagull drool!

P.P.P. needed the girl to find her and pick her up. The girl needed P.P.P. and her good luck. Would they ever find each other again?

On the way home from school, the girl's shoelace came untied. "More bad luck," she thought. But when she bent down to tie it, what did she see? A penny! Not just any penny, but Pretty Patty Penny! This time she put Patty in her <u>other</u> pocket, with no hole in it. She ran all the way home and put Patty in her piggy bank. She never had bad luck again, and neither did Pretty Patty Penny.

P.U.!

OUCH!

Help! Find me! Pick me up!

And I don't mean a stupid seagull!

Leah just passed me a note. It says:

What are you writing about? When can I see your notebook? I'll show you mine.

(P.S. Mine is full of secrets.)

    I just don't know if I should show her. It's hard to decide. Some things should just be for yourself, but some are okay to share with your best friend. Some things are even better when you share them, like Space World. Maybe I should just show her already. Especially if she shows me hers.

Some things just go together, like:

salt and pepper

ham and eggs

peanut butter and jelly

Leah and me

Nadia and me

I have an idea! When I was 9, I only wrote stories by myself. Now I'm 1 0, so it's time for a change— I'll write a story UNDER Leah IN MY NOTEBOOK!

bad drawing of pointing hand — I know Leah can draw it better

Leah—you can see what's in my notebook by writing in it yourself. Let's do a story together. Here!

Amelia— Great idea! Here's the first sentence of our story.

There once was a boy named Nick who had a terrible secret.

He wrote about his secret in his notebook.

His best friend, George, begged and begged to read the notebook.

please! please! please!

please! please! please!

Finally, Nick said, "Okay. Here." But he was afraid of what George would think of his secret.

George was glad that Nick trusted him with his secret. He didn't think it was terrible at all!

Nick felt better having someone else know his secret and still like him.

The secret was

that Nick had a tail!

useful for picking things up and carrying them

And that's the end

of this tale!

I like the story Leah and I wrote together. So does she. And now she knows the kind of things I write in here. Maybe I'll show her the rest someday. I guess she felt left out when I wouldn't show her anything. I didn't mean to leave her out. She is my best friend, after all.

But I still worry that if she read what I wrote about numbers and hands, she might think I'm ~~weird~~ ~~wierd~~ ~~weird~~ ~~wierd~~ weird.

I give up! whichever way I write this word, it still looks ~~weird~~ ~~wierd~~ ~~weird~~ ~~wierd~~ weird!

I wonder what Leah thinks about and what she writes in her notebook.

Leah thinking about all the good stuff in her own notebook

Now I'm sure that things are okay between us because when Leah saw me staring at her, she asked, "What are you staring at? Do I have something on my face?"

"Yes," I said, and she started wiping her nose and mouth. "Yes!" I said. "Your nose! Your nose is on your face!" And I showed her the picture I drew of her. She laughed! She's a good friend, alright. Maybe I'll show her my <u>next</u> notebook.

BEEP! BEEP! LAST PAGE ALERT — TIME FOR A NEW NOTEBOOK! OH, CLEEEE — 00!

BEEEEEP